Good Night, Big Max

by Karen McDonald

ISBN: 979-8-9883743-2-9 (Ebook)
ISBN: 979-8-9883743-0-5 (Paperback)
ISBN: 979-8-9883743-1-2 (Cardboard)

Illustrated by Marlon at GetYourBookIllustrations
Book Design by Kezia at GetYourBookIllustrations
www.getyourbookillustrations.com

First Print 2023

To Tom, Emily, Lily and Caleb

Special Thanks to Marlon and the team at
GetYourBookIllustrations

Big Max, Big Max, It is time for bed.
Where will you lay your big, sleepy head?
In your kennel?

No, no, not in my kennel.
The hard plastic floor will make my body sore.

Big Max, Big Max, It is time for bed.
Where will you lay your big, sleepy head?
On the brown couch?

No, no, not on the brown couch.
It is too hard to climb and will take
too much time.

Big Max, Big Max, it is time for bed.
Where will you lay your big, sleepy head?
On your cat bed?

No, no, not on my cat bed.
It is too tiny for my heinie,
and my head will hang out.

Big Max, Big Max, it is time for bed.
Where will you lay your big, sleepy head?
On the fancy crushed velvet couch?

No, no, not on the fancy crushed velvet couch.
Even though it feels like a feather,
it is off limits to me, and I know better.

Big Max, Big Max, it is time for bed.
Where will you lay your big, sleepy head?

On the long, green couch in the garage?

No, no, not on the long, green couch in the garage. I am too scared to sleep alone in the dark. I will stay up all night and BARK, BARK, BARK, BARK!

Big Max, Big Max, it is time for bed.
Where will you lay your big, sleepy head?
Outside on your hammock?

No, no, not outside on my hammock.
I like watching the squirrels scamper and run,
but being alone would not be fun.

Big Max, Big Max, it is time for bed.
Where will you lay your big, sleepy head?
In Papa G and Mama K's big bed?

Yes! Yes! That is the perfect place to lay my big, sleepy head and go to bed!

But, Big Max, the big bed is too tall.

When you climb up on it, you might fall.

Then where, oh where,
can I lay my big, sleepy head?

How about in your very own bed,
next to Papa G and Mama K's bed.

Yes! Yes! My very own bed! That is the perfect place to lay my big, sleepy head.

Good night, Big Max.

Wait!!! Can I have a Big Mac Snack Attack snack and a big, wet kiss on the lips?

YUM!
SMACK!

SNACK!
ATTACK!

Good night, Big Max.

Big Max Challenge

Big Max wants his own bedroom. He needs your help designing it. Draw and label a dream bedroom for Big Max. DM a picture of your creation to Big Max's Instagram: **bigmaxgentlegiant** for a chance to have your design posted on his site!

Thank you!

Thanks for reading Good Night, Big Max.
Please leave a review on Amazon and check out
Big Max A True Story available on Amazon in paperback or kindle.
Visit Karen at her website: **karenmcdonaldauthor.com**